Ø

#ONWARD!

VOLUME 1

SCOT STREET STYLE

A SCOT STREET STYLE book

ISBN 978-0-9932826-0-7

PRINTED BY BIDDLES BOOKS

The publishers policy is to use papers and products that are natural, renewable and recyclable and made from wood grown in sustainable forests. The logging and manufacturing processes are expected to conform to the environmental regulations. This books is printed on FSC paper.

Scot Street Style Ltd Reg. No. SC84513
14 Eskview Grove, Dalkeith, Midlothian, EH22 1JW

www.ScotStreetStyle.com

Editor-in-Chief	Creative Director	Logo & Interior Design	Cover Image
Crawford Coutts	Gordon J Millar	Supermark	David Boni

Ø

#ONWARD!

VOLUME 1

"Being part of this community seems to invigorate your creative juices, and gets people who were perhaps hesitant at first, to take that business plunge"

-

SCOTT MCLACHLAN

―――

"What I love about Scot Street Style is how it brings together people from all over Scotland who share a love for creativity and gives us the chance to celebrate it together. It doesn't matter what your specific artistry is, it is a celebration of all things creative… and a celebration of Scotland itself!"

-

ANNA MCLUCKIE

―――

"It's like a long lost energy. It's made me fall back in love with creativity and creative people"

-

JULIAN KYNASTON

"Scot Street Style is an ever expanding horizon of diversity. Whilst we embrace our heritage, a new wave of cultural influence has diversified and evolved Scotland's style"

-

JAMIE C JOHNSTONE

"Scot Street Style is a way of thinking. It is an acceptance and curiosity to find, try and share new things, with new people. Scot Street Style is not defined by the aesthetic or look of a typical subculture or movement, it is defined by a shared value and ethos of community, shared experience and continual growth"

-

ALAN MOORE

"A platform that supersedes the established closed doors of fashion and style"

-

MARK HOGARTH

SPECIAL THANKS & MENTIONS

A huge thank you to every single person who pledged to our crowdfunding campaign for the publication of this book, and to those who supported us: The Bearded Bastard, Bonnie Bling, Outsiders Apparel, Naromode, Abandon Ship Apparel, Tens, Christine Clark & Judy R Clark, Dauvit Alexander (Justified Sinner), Hatti Pattisson and Simon Murphy.

To our incredible team behind the scenes: Supermark, Betty and Bee, Chris Clark and Louise Clark, we couldn't have done this without you.

A special mention to Boombarbers, Illamasqua, Scotland Re:Designed and Rebel Rebel who drove this dream onward to the finish line and beyond.

To all the contributors who shared their time, energy and passion in this book, and to all the bloggers, likers and tweeters for your support, thank you.

To David Boni for the cover shot, my gratitude is infinite.

Without Victor Spence, His Holiness the Dalai Lama, the World Peace Tartan and Bill Cunningham, there would be no Scot Street Style, thank you from the bottom of my heart.

And to Crawford Coutts for believing, we did it, thank you. Onward!

Gx

Introduction:

COMMUNITY, CONNECTIVITY, CURATION

A showcase of the amazingly diverse and vibrant creative community of Scotland. Capturing the essence of Scottish style, character and humour by transforming social media into social reality. Promoting Scottish design and artistic innovation to draw the eyes of the world to this land and what it means to be Scottish in the 21st Century.

Social media is a wonderful tool, we can find pretty much anybody and anything: our closest friends living on the other side of the world, work colleagues we see every day, our heroes, our aspirations, our inspirations.

There is the ability to connect, to build communities, and create world-changing products and services with people we could never have imagined would be in our social or work networks.

To aide us on our quest to reinvigorate the perception of Scotland throughout the world across Social Media and Social Reality, we began connecting like-minded individuals and started to build a community. We hosted events called "The Gathering" throughout Scotland and from all of this we curated the most driven new innovators in the country and put them together in this tangible high quality hardback book.

When an idea galvanises a global community, a movement is born... From Midlothian to Manhattan, we want to share our incandescent creative flame with the whole world. 2014 was a historic year for Scotland with the Commonwealth Games and the referendum on independence but there is no end point to what we have started here.

We want to raise aspirations, smash negative stereotypes, and strive unremittingly to achieve our potential as human beings. And we will not rest until our cities are mentioned in the same breath as Milan, Tokyo, London, Paris, New York...

Onward!

G

———

Gordon J Millar, Creative Director of Scot Street Style Ltd.
A family man, currently working full time as a nurse. He has a background in
building peace and environmental social media communities, including
working with His Holiness the Dalai Lama and Arun Gandhi.

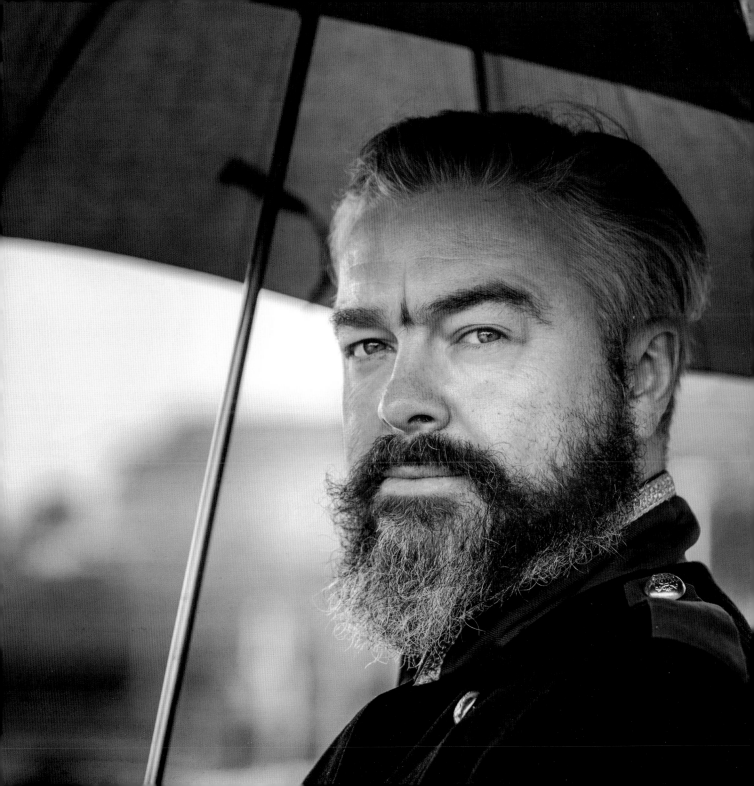

SCOT STREET STYLE

——

Where it all began...

WORLD PEACE TARTAN

———

In the beginning...

In late 2011 and up to June 2012 Gordon Millar was part of a fantastic team of people that I had the privilege to lead in delivering a historic visit to Scotland by His Holiness The Dalai Lama. In the years immediately leading up to this visit the World Peace Tartan was born. The gestation period of this new contemporary 'Tartan with Purpose' went all the way back to December 1999 when I first met with The Dalai Lama in Cape Town, South Africa.

Such a tartan derives its potential through bringing together a powerful message for peace from the heart of Scotland woven to

the knowledge that tartan is a globally recognised cultural icon that happens to be an amazing platform for narratives of meaning. The World Peace Tartan was blessed with its launch in Scotland with His Holiness The Dalai Lama at packed and unforgettable public events in Edinburgh, Dundee and Inverness on the 22nd and 23rd of June 2012 with Gordon Millar being the 'live' and present social networker for the whole visit programme. The humble excited sense of privilege written all over Gordon's face was a joy to behold.

In April of 2013 the World Peace Tartan initiative moved on to New York City for the 2013 Tartan Week. Gordon was part of a small group that included Louise to support the @PeaceTartan

mission. Louise ran the Central Park 10k while wearing the peace tartan by way of a sash. Gordon had already obtained a pair of what I would call powerfully visible World Peace Tartan trousers. These 'powerfully visible' trousers are infact a very important part of #scotstreetstyle history!

Key parts of the World Peace Tartan presence in New York Tartan week include Gordon and Louise wearing it on the Tartan Day Parade down 6th Avenue while carrying the American-Scottish Foundation banner with a group of young children from the New York Metro Pipeband family behind them all wearing the @PeaceTartan scarves.

Next was the formal US launch of the World Peace Tartan with Arun Gandhi, the Grandson of Mahatma Gandhi, wearing our first kilt states-side on the catwalk of the 'Dressed to Kilt' Fashion Show in New York along with a gorgeous World Peace Tartan 'frock coat' by the inspirational and greatly talented Judy R Clark. These were amazing moments that the UK and US media took a great interest in that included the New York Times, The Times, The Herald and front page photo coverage in The Scotsman as well as inside page coverage for Judy's signature creation.

The third and key element was the moment when Gordon and Louise were together enjoying a walk in New York still wearing their World Peace Tartan when they were approached by an enquiring man on a push bike carrying a camera in his bag. He wanted to know about the radiating tartan and these two young gorgeous people wearing it so Gordon and Louise shared the story. This enquiring man unbeknown to Gordon and Louise at the time was the living legend New York Times photographer of New York street style Mr Bill Cunningham! He asked to take their photo which they were very happy to accommodate and then the rest is history. #scotstreetstyle was born that day thanks to synchronicity.

With the seeds being planted that day in April 2013 in Manhattan, New York and being wonderfully nurtured and cultivated with Gordon's then released and channelled creativity, along with an unfolding vision, passion and commitment, a wonderful and truly exciting movement with a purpose came to life that now involves thousands of people. If #scotstreetstyle isn't a powerful creative 'happening' I don't know what is! All who view, read and enjoy all the amazing contributions in this precious book are experiencing the manifestation of a great gift of cause and effect! Enjoy! Be inspired! Spread the positive creative energy! Inspire others! Be the change you wish to see in the world!

#Onward!

BY VICTOR SPENCE
FOUNDER OF THE WORLD PEACE TARTAN INITIATIVE
VISIT CO-ORDINATOR IN SCOTLAND FOR HIS HOLINESS THE DALAI LAMA
CULTURAL DIPLOMAT AND PEACE ACTIVIST

#ONWARD!

VOLUME 1

GREIG PATERSON

MODEL

———

I first met the man behind Scot Street Style quite by chance at a Movember event in Edinburgh's Harvey Nics, I said "hi" in the passing not knowing who he was or what he represented other than another nice bearded fellow who had come along to join in.

It wasn't long afterwards that I was signed to one of Scotland's top modelling agencies and as an electrical engineer from Alloa, modelling seemed like a big world I knew nothing about. I subsequently joined up to Instagram as a way to share my work and try to find photographers and maybe people in the same boat.

It was here I came across the Scot Street Style page and recognised the man I met the previous November. From there I was instantly connected to hundreds of designers, photographers, models and creatives alike. I have since connected, met and worked with some of the nicest, most talented people in the country and without which I wouldn't have known where to start.

I feel I owe a lot to this man, who we all look up to and has made us all feel part of something much larger than any of our individual careers and we've all come to know him affectionately as just 'G'.

TRISTAN CAMERON-HARPER

MODEL AND PRO ICE HOCKEY PLAYER

———

Whatever you do never ever give up, always take advice onboard & most importantly enjoy what your doing.

———

 @tristancameronharper

PHOTOGRAPH BY TOM CAIRNS

JONATHAN DANIEL PRYCE

AWARD WINNING STREET AND FASHION PHOTOGRAPHER

———

Freedom, creativity and individuality. Believing in your own voice and connecting with others of like mind.

———

 @GarconJon

MODELS: DANNY SCRIMSHAW AND JOHN MORRIS
LOCATION: EDINBURGH

ALAN MOORE

AWARD WINNING DESIGNER AT TEN30 FASHION

———

You will find yourself in some of the most amazing situations, in places you never imagined, with people you will love, all because you have that creativity within your soul.

———

 @ten30fashion

PHOTOGRAPH BY DAVID STANTON
MODEL: JOHN O' HAGAN
LOCATION: ISLE OF KERRERA
JACKET BY ALAN MOORE
COMPANY: TEN30

GARY SCOTT

GLASGOW BASED FILM BLOGGER

———

Do something because you have to. Stay honest, stay hungry and stay focused.

———

 *@troublewithfilm*

PHOTOGRAPH BY LYNSAY NEIL
T-SHIRT BY ABANDON SHIP APPAREL

LYNSAY NEIL

LIPSTICK LOVER, TATTOO GIGGLER AND WEARER OF BOWS

———

Be yourself. Blaze your trail and don't be afraid if what you're doing is a little different. Never forget that you can do anything, you gorgeous creature!

———

 *@misswestendgirl*

JUDY R CLARK

AWARD WINNING FASHION DESIGNER

———

Dreams are very important and sometimes quite extraordinary, I feel they should be treasured and shared with the ones you are close to.

———

 @judyrclark1

DAVID MOFFATT

PHOTOGRAPHER AND MUSICIAN

———

Always treat people with respect and remember that whatever someone chooses to wear or how they look is never as important as their words, actions and attitude.

———

@moffphotography

PHOTOGRAPH BY DAVID MOFFATT
MODEL: HOLLIE ELLA BURGOYNE

NEXT PAGE:
PHOTOGRAPH BY DAVID MOFFATT
LOCATION: T IN THE PARK

KESTIN HARE

CREATIVE DIRECTOR AT KESTIN HARE

———

Work together and help each other, rather than working against each other - Scotland is a small place!

———

 @kestinhare

PHOTOGRAPH BY DENNIS MCINALLY
COMPANY: KESTIN HARE
LOCATION: STOCKBRIDGE, EDINBURGH

OBSCURE COUTURE

UNIQUE STREET/STAGEWEAR FOR THE INTROVERTED EXTROVERT

———

Live fast, stay weird!

———

@obscure_couture

PHOTOGRAPH BY LIAM DICKSON

NEXT PAGE:
PHOTOGRAPH BY LIAM PERKINS

LEYAH SHANKS

FOUNDER OF THE BODY CONFIDENCE REVOLUTION BLOG

———

Go for it. You never know what might happen until you try. Never give up!

———

 *@IAMLEYAHSHANKS*

PHOTOGRAPH BY MALIK TOG
MODEL: LEYAH SHANKS
DRESS: LADY JOJO'S BOUTIQUE

DOMINIC MARTIN

FREELANCE PHOTOGRAPHER

———

Don't ask, don't get. Be ever vigilant of opportunities and take every chance you get to practice what you love.

———

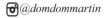 *@domdommartin*

PHOTOGRAPH BY DOMINIC MARTIN
MODEL: VICTORIA MIDDLETON

SALLY-ANN PROVAN
DESIGNER AND MILLINER

———

Don't. Give. Up.

———

@*sallyannhats*

PHOTOGRAPH BY ALISTAIR CLARK PHOTOGRAPHY
MODEL: NEVE CAFFREY

KERRY LYTWYN
PHOTOGRAPHER

———

Follow your dreams but most of all follow your heart and never give in to society's pressures and constraints.

———

@*kerrylytwyn*

MODEL: KERRY LYTWYN

PHOTOGRAPH BY KERRY LYTWYN
MODEL: ADRIAN BERNAL, BOOKINGS MODELS, LONDON

BENJAMIN PATCHETT

GENTLEMEN'S HAIRCUTS

———

Work hard every day and continue building a strong reputation.

———

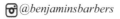 *@benjaminsbarbers*

PHOTOGRAPH BY MARK PATCHETT
LOCATION: STOCKBRIDGE, EDINBURGH
COMPANY: BENJAMIN'S BARBER SHOP

PETER MCNALLY

PICTURE MAKER

———

Create for yourself.

———

@petermcnally

PHOTOGRAPH BY PETER MCNALLY
MODEL: STEFANIA
LOCATION: MEADOWS, EDINBURGH

JAWN MCCLENAGHAN
GLASGOW BASED PHOTOGRAPHER

———

Do your best at all times and constantly progress in your field, when the right person does come along, you'll be ready for the next step.

———

COLIN MCANDREW

MANAGING DIRECTOR AT MEDUSA HAIR

———

Work hard acknowledge those who have helped you then share back.

———

@*colinmcandrew*

COMPANY: MEDUSA HAIR
PHOTOGRAPH BY CJ MONK

ZENO WATSON

PHOTOGRAPHER

———

Stay positive and be yourself, believe in what you do and treat others the way you like to betreated.

———

 @zenowatson

Ø

GARY CASSIDY

BEARD AMBASSADOR AND MODEL

———

Be yourself, embrace your differences, and always remember that you are good enough!

———

@consciousgary

PHOTOGRAPH BY ISTVAN JANCSO

PHOTOGRAPH BY CALUM MCKENZIE
COMPANY: BRAW BEARD OILS

FIONA SOMERVILLE

DESIGNER

———

Don't give up, it takes a long time but you won't be poor forever.

———

@fionasomervilledesign

ALL GARMENTS DESIGNED AND MADE BY
FIONA SOMERVILLE
PHOTOGRAPH BY ANDREW MOOR

ROBERT FRANCE

DUNDEE BASED PHOTOGRAPHER

@still2click

CHRISTIAN MACLEOD

AWARD WINNING ACCESSORY DESIGNER

—

Work incredibly hard into getting your product to speak, let your product do all the talking for you.

—

 *@christianmacleod*

PHOTOGRAPH BY JOHN PAUL
MODELS: KIT WILLIAMS, JAMES SUTTON, STEPHEN
BILLINGTON & CHRISTIAN MACLEOD
COMPANY: CHRISTIAN MACLEOD

MARK BRADLEY

INDEPENDENT MEN'S WEAR DESIGNER

———

Discover what you love, don't hide it or lock it away. Embrace what makes you happy and discover how to make it work for you.

———

 @G69clothing

KARLIE WU

STREET STYLE PHOTOGRAPHER, STUDYING AT GLASGOW SCHOOL OF ART

———

Don't stop what you're doing, you're doing great. Perseverance is key.

———

@glaswegianwestwood

DAUVIT ALEXANDER

METALSMITH WORKING IN GLASGOW

———

A carefully-placed business card and a few memorable words can make people take note and remember you. Being kind and generous is a good way to start.

———

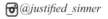 *@justified_sinner*

PORTRAIT OF DAUVIT ALEXANDER, THE JUSTIFIED SINNER
PHOTOGRAPH BY SIMON MURPHY, 2012

PIECE TITLE: KO SI IRUUFEN MADE BY DAUVIT ALEXANDER
PHOTOGRAPH BY SIMON MURPHY, 2014
MODEL - KIRSTIN NORMA BEATON
MAKE-UP AND HAIR - SAM HENDRY

JULIAN KYNASTON

FOUNDER OF ILLIMASQUA AND PROPAGANDA

———

Think big.

———

@JulianKynaston

PHOTOGRAPH BY EDDIE MONSOON
COMPANY: ILLAMASQUA & PROPAGANDA UKT

KAREN SMITH
JEWELLERY DESIGNER AND MAKER

———

Do what you love and never give up, but most of all believe in yourself!

———

@kasjewellery

PHOTOGRAPH BY ROSIE ANDERSON
COMPANY: KAREN SMITH JEWELLERY & METAL DESIGN

MARK HOGARTH

CREATIVE DIRECTOR OF HARRIS TWEED HEBRIDES

———

Listen and learn. Perfect the product before the grand unveiling

———

@hogarthism

Ø

DARYL GILLESPIE
BONAFIDE BARBER

——

Do it. Don't go in blind. You need as much logic as love but don't let one outweigh the other. If you want it you definitely can.

——

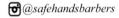 *@safehandsbarbers*

PHOTO BY RYAN CAMPBELL PHOTOGRAPHY
MODELS: GRAEME MACASKILL & DARYL GILLESPIE
COMPANY: SAFE HAND BARBERS

VICKY VIOLA

RETRO STYLE ROCKABILLY BLOGGER

———

In the words of Dr Seuss, why fit in when you were born to stand out?

———

@*MissVickyViola*

PHOTOGRAPH BY KERRY MURRAY

WENDY H GILMOUR

FASHION STYLE AND LIFE BLOGGER

———

Work hard. Nothing amazing ever comes easy but when it's something you really truly love, your passion will shine through if you just keep going.

———

 @thankfifi

RABBIE DENIM

UNIQUE WORLD CLASS CUSTOM MADE JEANS

———

Time awaits no man, but it also takes time for your work to become as unique as the creative who's creating it. So bide your time.

JEREMY WESTACOTT

BEARDED CANADIAN IN SCOTLAND

———

Don't be afraid to push yourself outside of your comfort zones, meet new people and engage with communities that have similar passions and creative desires as you do.

———

@jeremymichaelwestacott

LUCY CONNELLY

PERSONAL STYLE BLOGGER

———

Take the leap of faith, whatever your passion may be, take the initiative and make the most of every opportunity.

———

 @lucyflorals

PHOTOGRAPH BY CHRISTOPHER ALLAN

JILL SKULINA

VISUAL ARTIST, MOTHER, CREATOR, AND JACKETEER

———

Keep going, regularly reflect on your work, ditch what doesn't work for you, move forward and most importantly enjoy what you do.

———

 @jillskulina

PHOTOGRAPH BY ZOE BARRIE
FROM PHOTOS BY ZOE

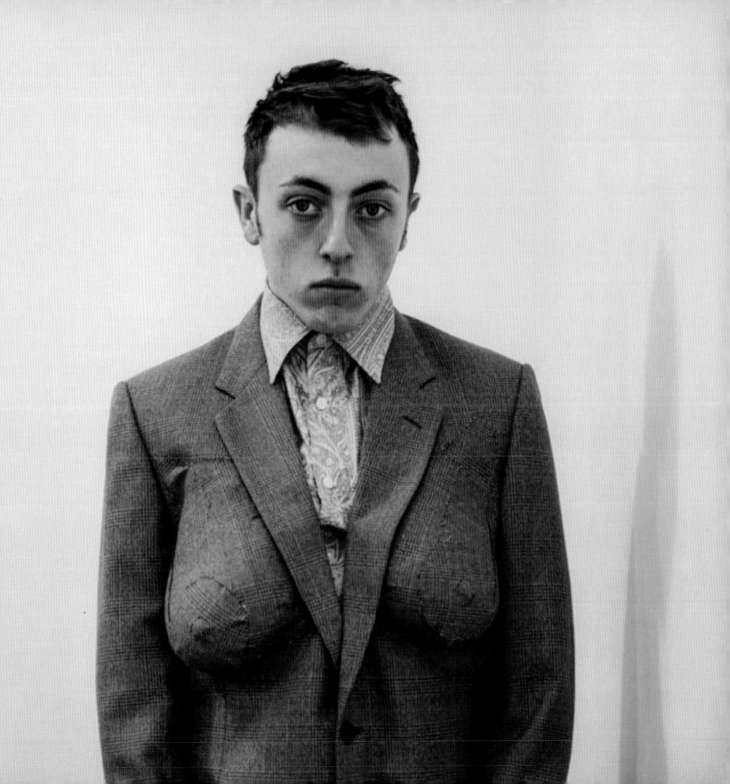

AYMEE CHARLTON

FASHION DESIGNER

———

If you really want something, don't stop until you get it.
With smart thinking and patience you can reach your own goal.

———

 @aymeejo

PHOTOGRAPH BY NATALIE BAXTER
MODEL: ANNA MCLAUGHLIN
COMPANY: AYMEE CHARLTON

NICOLA GARDENER

WOMAN'S WEAR DESIGNER/DIRECTOR

———

Do as much research as possible in your chosen field and attend lots of networking events, seminars and work-shops. Be prepared to work hard to achieve your goal and do not give up easily as it is truly rewarding when all your hard work pays off!

———

 *@nicci_n_*

PHOTOGRAPH BY VINCENT LAMB
COMPANY: NICCI.N.

GREG MILNE

STYLIST AND MODEL

———

Collaborate, think what you can bring that isn't already being done. Don't shy away from things that you may deem to be cool, a commercial job probably has a lot of great lessons that you can then utilise when creating something more artistic.

———

@greg_milne

PHOTOGRAPH BY VICTOR ALBROW
MODEL: GREG MILNE
CLOTHES: WE LOVE TO BOOGIE

WARDROBE CONVERSATIONS

BLOGGERS

———

Reach out to others - we are all in the same boat and we are a lovely bunch!

———

 @wardrobeconversations

TOM CAIRNS

CAPTURING ORDINARY MOMENTS IN TIME, AND TURNING THEM INTO EXTRA ORDINARY IMAGES

———

When you have a passion for something you have to follow it and have no reservations or regrets....but what a difference it can make to you and others.

———

 @tomcairns

RYAN MCMAHON

MODEL, MUSICIAN AND SALSA LOVER

———

Be proactive; surround yourself with people that want to see you succeed, never put anyone else down, always ask advice from those that have been and done it before you and, most importantly, stay humble.

———

@ryanmaximillianmcmahon

PHOTOGRAPH BY GABRIELA SILVEIRA
MAKE UP & HAIR: JAK MORGAN
STYLING: STEFANIE OLIVIA SNEDDON

Ø

AMANDA DAVIES

PASTEL LOVING STYLE BLOGGER

———

Do what you love and don't change yourself or your style just to get more readers/likes/follows, the creative industry is all about individuality, don't become the clone of someone else because only you can be you.

———

 @honey_pop

CRAIG LOWE

FREE THINKING RENEGADE

———

Believe in your dreams and passions. Allow yourself to be yourself, it's good to be different and once you let yourself follow your own path, like minded people will always appear from somewhere to help.

———

@iamcraig23

———

PHOTOGRAPH BY LOUISE MATHER
& NO MIDDLE NAME CREATIVE

AIMEE PAGET

FASHION STUDENT AND DESIGNER

———

Do what you enjoy and do it for yourself. Don't be scared to do.

———

@never_monday

PHOTOGRAPH BY ALEX ADAIR
MODELS: MORGAN POPE AND TAMZIN O'MALLEY
MAKE UP: ANGELA SINCLAIR

EMMA MCPHERSON
DESIGNER AND MANUFACTURER OF DANDY NEEDS AND TWEEDS

———

Work with as many companys as possible in lots of different roles. Be willing to give up your social life to work long hours and weekends to get your dream... Never give up on a dream!!

———

 @buckandhare

PHOTOGRAPH BY IAN DOCHERTY
MODEL: DANNY SCRIMSHAW
COMPANY: BUCK & HARE

CALUM MCKENZIE

PORTRAIT/FASHION PHOTOGRAPHER

———

Believe in yourself, push yourself to achieve what you want to do. Keep yourself busy, make something of it!

———

@kenziexphotography

STEWART BRYDEN

INTERNATIONALLY PUBLISHED PHOTOGRAPHER (BA)

———

Hone your skills to where you feel remotely ready. Don't be afraid to make mistakes, but when you do, apologise to the client, you will learn more from a mistake than you will from recurring success.

———

 @stewbryden

Ø

MARTIN WATKINS

BRINGING THE OLD SCHOOL TO THE NEW SCHOOL IN MEN'S GROOMING

———

Follow your dreams don't just think about it... Get up and do it for the love and passion and not the money.

———

 @the_dapper_gent

PHOTOGRAPH BY CJ MONK
PICTURED L TO R: MARTIN WATKINS, SCOTT MALONE
COMPANY: THE DAPPER GENT

NATALIE BAXTER

STUDENT AND FASHION PHOTOGRAPHER

———

Work with loads of different people to get recognised and its also lots of fun. Be yourself and have your own style don't try and copy other people.

———

PAUL SMITH

PHOTOGRAPHY STUDENT, ABERDEEN

———

Keep believing that your dreams can come true. With hard work and determination anything is possible.
Don't let people tell you what you can or cannot achieve in life.
If you put your mind to something then you will achieve.

———

KATIE JEFFERY

EDINBURGH BASED PHOTOGRAPHER

———

Never give up on what you love and never lose your passion for what got you started in the first place.

———

IAIN MACDONALD

AWARD WINNING DESIGNER

Get involved with the community and never give up trying to reach your goal, support each other and collaborate when you can, unfriendly rivalry benefits no one, encourage each other.

 @naromode

PHOTOGRAPH BY CAMERON HENDERSON
MODEL: LAURIE DUFFY
COMPANY: NAROMODE

PHOTOGRAPH BY CAMERON HENDERSON
MODEL: LAURIE DUFFY
COMPANY: NAROMODE

CJ MONK
CONCEPT ARTIST AND PHOTOGRAPHER

@cj_monk

BEHN CROSS

BARBER AND MUSICIAN

———

When everyone else tells you no, simply just take them on, on your own cause shy kids get nothing.

PHOTOGRAPH BY DAVID MUIR
MODEL: BEHN CROSS
WEARING SF BRAND

CAMERON TAYLOR

SCOTTISH CONTEMPARY KNITWARE

@_cameron_taylor

PHOTOGRAPH BY CAMERON HENDERSON
MAKE UP: KATIE CONNELLY
MODEL: TALLULAH JARDIN
COMPANY: CAMERON TAYLOR

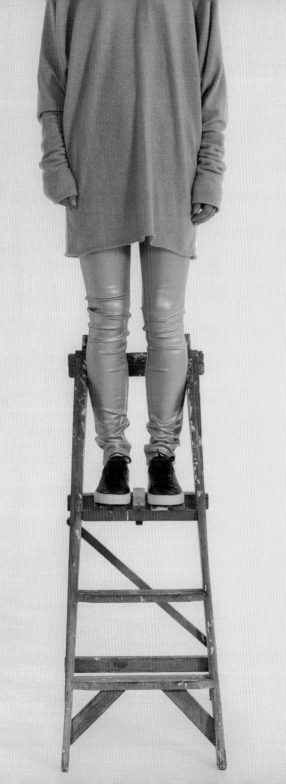

Ø

CHRISTINA MILLER

LIFE AND STYLE WRITER/BLOGGER

———

Have faith and never, ever give up. Your dreams are everything.

———

 *@the_daydreamer_*

CLAIRE PATERSON

EDINBURGH VINTAGE BOUTIQUE

———

Be brave, take the leap and do what you love doing, you'll be much happier for it! Do it!

———

@thosewerethedaysvintage

ROY ROGERS
HAIRDRESSER

———

Share ideas meet new friends and be inspired

———

📷 *@Milk_Hairdressing*

PHOTOGRAPH BY PAUL MARR
HAIR BY ROY ROGERS
COMPANY: MILK HAIRDRESSING

MR CLARK & MR TIMMS

FOUNDERS OF P&CO

———

Every day should be exciting, if it's not - you're doing it wrong.

———

 @pandco

PHOTOGRAPH BY GOBINDER JHITTA
MODEL: RICKI HALL (NEVS)
LOCATION: THE COMPOUND, BIRMINGHAM, UK
CLOTHING: P&CO

ISLAY SPALDING

DESIGNER AND MAKER OF CONTEMPORARY JEWELLERY

———

Work hard, ask questions, always learn and remember to be yourself.

———

@islayspalding

PALOMA FERNANDEZ

EDINBURGH BASED FASHION PHOTOGRAPHER

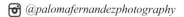

📷 *@palomafernandezphotography*

PHOTOGRAPH BY PALOMA FERNANDEZ
MODEL: NIKITA COJÉ @MODEL TEAM
MUA: RONA SKUODAS
WARDROBE STYLIST: LAURA VILLANUEVA

PHOTOGRAPH BY PALOMA FERNANDEZ
MODELS: JODIE-ANN MCNEILL & MARLIES ROLAND
AT SUPERIOR MODEL MANAGEMENT
MUA AND HAIR: DANIELLE DICKSON

ELLIE MUNRO

PHOTOGRAPHER, WRITER AND PERPETUAL THRIFTER

———

From the outside, our community may seem daunting. However, as someone openly riddled with confidence and anxiety issues; the loving, supportive nature of Scot Street Style is often what keeps me from retreating into myself. It's a classroom of learning, and the door is always open.

———

 *@melancholyellie*

PHOTOGRAPH BY ELLIE MUNRO

PHOTOGRAPH BY ELLIE MUNRO

PHOTOGRAPH BY ELLIE MUNRO

DETROIT LAW

SINGER / GUITARIST FOR THE DUKE, DETROIT

———

Believe in what you do, work hard on your craft and never let anything compromise your art.

———

 @thedukedetroit

PHOTOGRAPH BY VICTORIA COATES
BAND: THE DUKE, DETROIT

REBECCA TORRES

AWARD WINNING READY-TO-WEAR LABEL

———

Go for it. It is hard to put yourself out there but if it is what you truly love and want to do then its worth it.

———

@ *@rebeccatorresofficial*

PHOTOGRAPH BY GORDON BURNISTON

DEBAY DeLUX
SHOWGIRL, TATTOO APPRENTICE AND MODEL

@debaydelux

JACQUELINE MARR

FIGURATIVE PAINTER, FINE ARTIST

———

Nourish the soul and take control.

ANDY BELL
PORTRAIT PHOTOGRAPHER EXTRAORDINAIRE

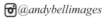

📷 *@andybellimages*

PHOTOGRAPH BY ANDY BELL
MODEL: CHRIS JOHN MILLINGTON

SUPERMARK

GLASGOW BASED BRAND, GRAPHIC AND SPACIAL DESIGNER

———

You can be anyone you want to be. Even yourself.

———

@*supermark_*

RICHARD DAVIES

OWNER OF ABANDON SHIP APPAREL, SLEEPING GODS, HARD GRIND DUNDEE AND PLUG AND STRING

———

It's really rather simple, be honest to yourself and your audience, do what you love and remain positive and focus on what you are doing, thats all that matters.

———

@rich_idlehands

———

SIMON MURPHY

PHOTOGRAPHER AND TEACHER

@smurph77

PHOTOGRAPH BY SIMON MURPHY
HIS HOLINESS THE DALAI LAMA
LOCATION: INVERNESS, SCOTLAND

PHOTOGRAPH BY SIMON MURPHY
MODEL: STEWART BRYDEN

GILLIAN MCBAIN
PHOTOGRAPHER, TALL. SCOTTISH. PRETTY EPIC.

———

Follow your instinct. There's something in there that wants to be seen, keep creating and let it out.

———

 @seethroughme

ANNA MCLUCKIE

HARPEE, SINGER, SONGWRITER

———

Share what you do with other people. Doing what you love for yourself feels good but doing it with other people feels so much better!

———

@annamcluckie

PHOTOGRAPH BY SEB SINGH

EMMA MCMAHON

FASHION DESIGNER / MAKER

———

Just go for it. Get involved, with community projects and be aware of the creatives around you.

———

@*aesirdesigner*

LOUISE ARNOT

FASHION BLOGGER FROM EDINBURGH

———

When creative opportunities come your way, take as many as you can as they can give you valuable insight and contacts. Plus you never know what those opportunities might lead to.

———

@LouLouBrooke

TARA NOWY

PROFESSIONAL MODEL AND COLUMNIST

———

Never give up. Often when you have your greatest doubts your largest door will open. Determination and positivity are key. Keep pushing.

———

 @taranowy

PHOTOGRAPH BY STEWART BRYDEN
HAIR AND MUA MOLLY SHERIDAN
CLOTHES: ARSALAN

LYNETTE GRAY

UNISEX BRAND DESIGNER

———

You will never please everyone but if you can inspire at least one person with what you are doing then it is worth it, even if that one person is you!

———

@angelpixielove

———

PHOTOGRAPH BY STUART IRVINE
COMPANY: ANGELPIXIELOVE (GIRLS) AND APL (BOYS)

ELAINE, ALAN & ANTONIO

CHAMPIONING EMERGING DESIGNERS

———

Be your own story.

———

@wearponymous

CLOTHING: NAROMODE
COMPANY : WEAR EPONYMOUS

BETTY & BEE

CREATIVE CONSULTANCY FOR FASHION, BEAUTY AND LIFESTYLE

——

Take your dreams into your own hands. If there is something you want to do, then do it!
Don't wait for someone to give you the opportunity, it wont happen.
If you are willing to learn, work hard and keep positive, the sky's the limit.

——

@foreveryoursbetty
@beewaits

ANN RUSSELL

FREELANCE WRITER, BLOGGER AND FASHION STYLIST

———

Surround yourself with inspirational people. Not just fellow creatives but friends and family that push you to be better. The beauty of being creative is that it encourages variety so embrace the success of your peers, collaborate with one another but also find the point of difference that makes your own work special.

———

 @FrockTrade

PHOTOGRAPH BY CHRIS PARK
STYLIST: ANN RUSSELL
MODEL: TARA NOWY
MAKE UP: CAROL FAIRFIELD

PHOTOGRAPH BY CHRIS BLOTT
STYLIST: ANN RUSSELL
HAIR AND MAKE UP: KIMBERLEY DEWAR
MODELS: AMANDA HENDRICK & FRED SZKODA

STEPH KELLY

DESIGNER AND STYLIST

———

Go for it, whatever your dream may be, life is too short not to. Believe in yourself, because if you believe that you can do it, then you can make any one else believe it too.

———

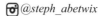 *@steph_abetwix*

PHOTOGRAPH BY HANNAH FORD
MODELS PAUL KEENAN AND ANNA FRENCH
DESIGNED BY STEPH KELLY

PHOTOGRAPH BY STEWART BRYDEN
SHOT FOR REBEL REBEL BARBERS
MODEL: LAUREN ELIZABETH ANDREW
STYLING: STEPH KELLY

DAVID MACLEOD

MODEL, SCHOOL TEACHER, COMPETITIVE BEARD GROWER

———

When I hear the words 'Scot Street Style' I am instantly reminded of the creativity, positivity, friendship and the memories that I've gained from being a part of this emerging global creative network, which embraces new talent, and nurtures so much potential. But above all, it means belonging to and being part of something much bigger than your self.

———

@davidjamesmacleod

PHOTOGRAPH BY RICHARD CRAIG
BESPOKE KILT DESIGN BY SIOBAHN MACKENZIE

MARIE OWEN

OWNER / DIRECTOR AT LOCATION SCOTLAND

WHAT DOES SCOT STREET STYLE MEAN TO YOU?

It's about gathering like minded, interesting and creative people from a broad range of backgrounds and with completely different thoughts on what style is. Get them in a room together and just see what happens, watch collaborations, ideas and partnership begin to grow in front of your eyes.

TELL US A BIT ABOUT YOUR CREATIVE JOURNEY SINCE OUR FIRST GATHERING LAST AUTUMN

I'm so lucky. My life, work and personal is enriched by the amount of interesting and inspiring people I meet on a regular basis I feel privileged to be able to be able to to to be part of their creative process and to personally learn from their experiences and style along the way. A personal high was working with photographer Peter Lindbergh earlier this year. His work is sensational and he was such a joy to work with. Very relaxed, approachable and put everyone in his presence at ease I really believe in what we at Location Scotland do. I'm so lucky to have a highly creative, focused and energetic team to believe in the LS ethos to get the global creative community to see what Scotland really has to offer.

MOVING ONWARD, WHAT ARE YOUR DREAMS AND ASPIRATIONS AS A CREATIVE?

I want to bring like minded, focused, ambitious and dedicated people together and help build a creative community that make people want to work in Scotland, not only for its beauty but for the wealth of fantastic people we have to offer here.

WHAT MESSAGE DO YOU HAVE FOR ASPIRING CREATIVES?

Just do it. If you truly believe in what you are doing and that's your passion you have to give it a go.

COMPANY: LOCATION SCOTLAND
ALL PHOTOGRAPHS BY LOCATION SCOTLAND

#ONWARD!

...to North America and Volume 2

JEREMIAH NEWTON

WONDERER AND COLLECTOR OF BEAUTIFUL SOULS

———

It is going to be tough, and with great success comes great failure, make sure to keep the good ones by your side, and lift up your friends when you do finally succeed, we are all in this struggle together!

———

 @tbbinc

COMPANY: THE BEARDED BASTARD

INFINITE GRATITUDE

———

Special thanks to...

REBEL REBEL

———

 @weerebel

———

WHAT DOES SCOT STREET STYLE MEAN TO YOU?

Scotland has rediscovered its passion. There's a growing community of people with new ideas & aspirations, who are more than willing to share their passion for their profession. Scot Street Style brings it all together.

TELL US A BIT ABOUT YOUR CREATIVE JOURNEY SINCE OUR FIRST GATHERING LAST AUTUMN

We have witnessed a transformation in our industry where fashion, hair trends and the clients thirst for variety and individualism are paramount... Since the autumn gathering the barbering movement has continued to see an increase in enthusiasm and energy, with the new wave of barbershops who actually give a feck about their trade. We need the barbering community to build on their skills and become more professional and stop acting like conveor belts who are content to chuck haircuts out. Our clients are style hungry and better educated about fashion and trends. They're emerging confident with their new style choice and more willing to share their new look on their smart phone. Clients like to be different and this allows us to add more passion and creativity to the movement that's sweeping Scotland. We've had the 'tatts on tour' boys in the shop right at the start of beard

phase when Chris Millington was bursting onto the scene. It was great fun welcoming them to Glasgow and we had small party in our barbershop... From that we got to meet Stew Bryden (model/photographer) who's just recently photographed our latest hair and fashion collection 'the kids we lost' and was in the January 2015 edition of "the modern barber".

MOVING ONWARD, WHAT ARE YOUR DREAMS AND ASPIRATIONS AS A CREATIVE?

We would love to work in collaboration with other creative parties to put on an annual eventin Scotland that celebrates the artists that live and work here; combining fashion, hair, tattoos, music, graffiti and more. We have so much talent in our lands it just needs a BIG platform.

WHAT MESSAGE DO YOU HAVE FOR ASPIRING CREATIVES?

Beauty is always in the eye of the beholder. Get off the fence and trust your own judgement. Be always open to new ideas, new people and get ready to embrace change. Always do the best job you can, because as a business you need to make a profit.

REBEL REBEL

PIONEERS OF BARBERING

SCOTT WILLIAMS

FOUNDER OF BOOMBARBERS

———

 @boombarbers

———

WHAT DOES SCOT STREET STYLE MEAN TO YOU?

Its about coming together and sharing a passion for all our crafts. A lot of people like to keep everything to themselves but by having Scot Street Style it allows one man or small band of creatives too join together and grow, share and build ideas.

TELL US A BIT ABOUT YOUR CREATIVE JOURNEY SINCE OUR FIRST GATHERING LAST AUTUMN

We have been working with people like Angelpixielove, Peiute, Outsiders Apparel along with Molly Sheridan and Dennis McInally. We launched our first ever Boombarbers Face of 2014 which was an awesome night won by David James Macleod.

MOVING ONWARD, WHAT ARE YOUR DREAMS AND ASPIRATIONS AS A CREATIVE?

Moving forward we at Boombarbers want and love to be part of a growing positive creative, helping young creatives to get experience, confidence and bring out the passion in Boombarbers.

WHAT MESSAGE DO YOU HAVE FOR ASPIRING CREATIVES?

My advice... work hard. Follow your Dreams. Share ideas. Listen to people that are doing it. But most of all, enjoy. Love your craft as this will shine through most of all.

PHOTOGRAPH BY DENNIS MCINALLY

MELVILLE
PLACE

boombarbers

boombarbers
20 1013

TIM STABLES

GLASGOW BASED BARBER IN TRAINING

———

WHAT DOES SCOT STREET STYLE MEAN TO YOU?

Scot Street Style has made me realise that it's ok to think different, not to go with the flow and to attempt to try out something new. It's an amazing feeling to know that you're not the only one trying to work out on something you love or would love to do. Having that support from your friends, loved ones and those you haven't had the pleasure of meeting, within the community, means a great deal and I don't believe I would have gone for my goal without it.

TELL US A BIT ABOUT YOUR CREATIVE JOURNEY SINCE OUR FIRST GATHERING LAST AUTUMN

2014 has been a crazy year for me. The referendum for Scottish Independence gave me a new passion, one I hope to see come to fruition in future. I got married to by best friend whom I love immensely. The day was perfect and couldn't have gone better. But I also ended up losing my job with Vodafone at the end of March. My attitude surprised me. I saw it as a chance to go for something new and get out of the "poisonous" and stereotypical office environment that just did nothing for me. In fact, it caused severe stress and anxiety. Since then, I have returned to college for an

evening course in Men's Barbery, become good friends with Mike Rice who cut my hair and now work along side him as a junior, learning what I can while attending college and cutting hair with his supervision. I feel like a new me. I realise this is a cliché to say such a thing, but I feel happier, more driven and I'm finally enjoying what is only the start of what I hope is a long and successful career.

MOVING ONWARD, WHAT ARE YOUR DREAMS AND ASPIRATIONS AS A CREATIVE?

I want to absorb as much info and good teachings as I can while maintaining the tempo of my practical practice. Quite frankly, I aim to be the best Barber in Scotland, if not the UK. I genuinely believe what I'm learning is a skill and I can't wait to see where it takes me.

WHAT MESSAGE DO YOU HAVE FOR ASPIRING CREATIVES?

Don't wait. Start today. You will be so much happier as a creative person for it, even if it's a small step, it's still a step forward. Speak to those involved, as many people as possible. Knowledge is invaluable power and you will never get enough of it.

COLIN GILCHRIST

DIGITAL MARKETING AT SOCIAL TAILOR. SCOTTISH FASHION BLOGGER. CREATIVE DIRECTOR SPENCER CLOTHING.

———

As a creative, I believe we are all artists. As artists I expect you to provide the unexpected, the scarce and the valuable.

———

 @colingilchrist

PHOTOGRAPH BY ANNA FREEMANTLE
COMPANY: SPENCER CLOTHING
DESIGNED BY COLIN GILCHRIST AND
DAWN M JONES

JANE DAVIDSON

DRESSING EDINBURGH SINCE 1969

@ *@janedavidson52*

QUEENE AND BELLE

INDEX

———

#ONWARD!

VOLUME 1